Tatsuki Fujimoto

I love chainsaws!

Tatsuki Fujimoto won Honorable Mention in the
November 2013 Shueisha Crown Newcomers' Awards for
his debut one-shot story *Love Is Blind*. His first series,
Fire Punch, ran for eight volumes. *Chainsaw Man* began
serialization in 2018 in *Weekly Shonen Jump*.

1

SHONEN JUMP Manga Edition

Story & Art TATSUKI FUJIMOTO

Translation/AMANDA HALEY
Touch-Up Art & Lettering/SABRINA HEEP
Design/JULIAN [JR] ROBINSON
Editor/ALEXIS KIRSCH

CHAINSAW MAN ⓒ 2018 by Tatsuki Fujimoto
All rights reserved.
First published in Japan in 2018 by SHUEISHA Inc., Tokyo.
English translation rights arranged by SHUEISHA Inc.

The stories, characters and incidents mentioned in this publication are entirely fictional.

Printed in Italy

Published by VIZ Media, LLC
P.O. Box 77010
San Francisco, CA 94107

20
First printing, October 2020
Twentieth printing, July 2024

PARENTAL ADVISORY
CHAINSAW MAN is rated T+ for Older Teen and is recommended for ages 16 and up. This volume contains violence and gore.

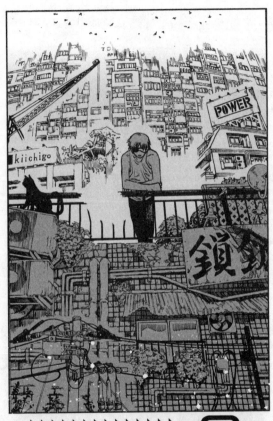

CHAINSAW MAN

1

DOG AND CHAINSAW

Tatsuki Fujimoto

CONTENTS

...1,200,000.

THE KIDNEY I JUST SOLD...

TREE-CUTTIN'...

SOLD ONE OF MY NUTS FOR...

HOW MUCH DID IT GO FOR AGAIN?

NOT EVEN 100,000?

...300,000.

MY RIGHT EYE...

...GETS ME 60,000 YEN A MONTH.

...38,040,000 YEN.

THAT BRINGS MY DEBT DOWN TOOOO...

LET'S GO KILL SOME-THING!

OKAY ALREADY, POCHITA. I KNOW!

Woof!

Chapter 1: Dog & Chainsaw

Chain saw man

IT'LL COME BACK FROM THE SEEDS, SO YOU SHOULD BURN IT.

THIS ONE'S A **TOMATO DEVIL,** SIR.

YOUR REWARD'S **400,000.**

THIS CORPSE'LL FETCH A HEFTY SUM ON THE BLACK MARKET.

GOOD JOB, DENJI.

ONLY 70,000 LEFT FOR ME...

WHICH IS 170,000 AFTER SUB-TRACTING YOUR DEBT AND INTEREST.

WOW, *THANKS!*

THEN AFTER TAKING OUT THE FINDER'S FEE, ET CETERA...

AFTER I USE THIS TO PAY THE WATER BILL...

I'M ALREADY DOWN TO 1,800 YEN...

THAT'S FUNNY.

PLUS THE DEBTS I'VE GOT TO OTHER PEOPLE...

WE HAVE TO LIVE ON THIS FOR THE REST OF THE MONTH...

GOT NOTHING TO EAT AT HOME...

OUR MEAL FOR THE DAY IS A SINGLE SLICE OF BREAD.

OKAY, POCHITA.

WHY ARE WE EMPLOYING SOME *KID* AS A DEVIL HUNTER?

MORE ACCURATELY, HIS WORTHLESS DEAD DAD'S DEBT.

WE'RE MAKING HIM PAY BACK HIS DEBT TO US.

PLUS, WHAT'S NICE ABOUT DENJI IS HE ALWAYS DOES AS HE'S TOLD.

IS A KID WITH A PET DEVIL REALLY FIT TO BE A DEVIL HUNTER?

NO DEVIL HUNTER WORTH THEIR SALT...

...WOULD DEAL DEAD DEVIL BODIES TO THE YAKUZA, NOW WOULD THEY?

NOW WE'LL BE ABLE TO EAT FOR THE NEXT *THREE DAYS!*

ZSSHHHH

WELL, "NORMAL" IS JUST A PIPE DREAM FOR US, ANYWAY.

FEELS LIKE I'LL BE PAYING OFF MY DEBT TILL THE DAY I DIE.

APPARENTLY, IT'S NORMAL TO EAT YOUR SLICED BREAD WITH JAM ON IT.

I HEARD SOMETHING RECENTLY...

Whiiiiine

AND I'LL PROLLY NEVER GET TO GO OUT WITH A GIRL.

CAN'T ASK A GIRL OVER TO MY RUN-DOWN SHACK, AND I DON'T GOT MONEY FOR A DATE EITHER.

IF DREAMS DO COME TRUE, I WANNA HUG A GIRL BEFORE I DIE...

ZSSSHHH

14

SSSShHHHH

BASTARD HUNG HIMSELF WITHOUT MAKING THIS MONTH'S PAYMENT...

KID... I DON'T CARE IF YOU BEG FOR IT OR WHORE YOURSELF OUT. HAVE 700,000 YEN READY BY TOMORROW.

OR I'LL CUT YOUR CORPSE INTO PIECES AND SELL YOU.

WHEN I CAN'T SLEEP, I THINK ABOUT MY DEBT, AND THEN IT'S EVEN HARDER TO FALL ASLEEP...

SO HUNGRY I CAN'T SLEEP...

OH, I KNOW...

THIS IS WHAT I'LL DREAM OF WHEN I FALL ASLEEP TONIGHT...

A DEVIL SHOWED UP *HERE*, SIR?

I DON'T SEE IT...

MAYBE IT HID SOME-WHERE?

OH, UH... YES, SIR...

DENJI, BOY... WE'RE GRATEFUL TO YOU, Y'KNOW.

UH-HUH...

...AND YOU WORK FOR CHEAP TREATS LIKE ONE TOO.

YOU'RE OBE-DIENT LIKE A DOG...

THING IS... I HATE DOGS. CAN'T STAND THE SMELL.

rst/

SHM

P

SO WE DECIDED TO DO LIKE YOU AND MAKE OUR OWN DEAL WITH A DEVIL.

WE WANTED TO GET STRONGER TOO. TO MAKE MORE MONEY.

WE YAKUZA BOYS...

YOU GUYS! CUT HIM INTO PIECES AND DUMP 'IM IN THE GARBAGE!

DEVIL HUNTERS KILL US DEVILS. I HATE THEM!!

SO I KILL THEM!

DAS

H

I MIGHT DIE WHILE I'M FIGHTING DEVILS.

POCHITA ---

THMP

THOM

Woof
!!!

POCHITA
...

DID YOU TAKE MY BODY? LIKE I TOLD YOU TO?

39

...SHOW ME YOUR DREAMS.

MY WOUNDS ARE GONE...

POCHITA!

WE CUT HIM TO RIBBONS AND HE'S STILL ALIVE?!

GROSS!

I *REALLY* HATE DEVIL HUNTERS!

HUH?

YOU GUYS!! EAT THAT FREAK!!

MAYBE I'M THE SAME.

BUT I STILL DREAMED OF A BETTER LIFE.

I SHOULDA BEEN HAPPY AS LONG AS I HAD POCHITA.

HOW COME THEY WANTED AN EVEN BETTER LIFE?

THESE GUYS ALREADY HAD PLENTY.

OH, I GET IT. EVERYBODY DREAMS. YOU CAN'T HELP IT.

THEN DREAMING'S NOT A BAD THING.

IT'S NOT A BAD THING, BUT...

HE *HAS* TO STAY DEAD IF WE EAT HIM...

GOT A LIVE ONE.

HMM...

IT ISN'T HUMAN *OR* DEVIL.

YOU HAVE A PECULIAR SMELL.

DID YOU DO THIS?

topple

HOLD ME...

H...

I CAME HERE TO KILL THE ZOMBIE DEVIL.

I'M A PUBLIC SAFETY DEVIL HUNTER.

YOU HAVE TWO CHOICES.

ONE, BE KILLED BY ME AS A DEVIL.

OR TWO, BE KEPT BY ME AS A HUMAN.

FOOD...?

WHAT WOULD I GET FOR BREAKFAST?

IF YOU'RE MY PET, I'LL GIVE YOU FOOD.

C
h
a
i
n
s
a
w

m a n

Chapter 2: The Place
Where Pochita Is

gurrrrigle

SORRY, UH... I'M BROKE...

THAT'S MY STOMACH...

LET'S GRAB SOME FOOD AT A REST STOP.

WE HAVEN'T HAD BREAKFAST EITHER.

PICK ANYTHING YOU WANT. I'LL PAY.

REALLY ?!

ALSO, YOU'LL DRAW ATTENTION SHIRTLESS. PUT THIS ON.

AND BY A PRETTY GIRL, AT THAT...

THIS'S THE FIRST TIME I'VE BEEN TREATED NICE.

PEOPLE ALWAYS CALL ME DIRTY AND SMELLY. NOBODY EVER COMES NEAR ME.

I'M IN LOVE.

SURE THING.

...A HOT DOG! IS THAT OKAY?!

OH, I'LL HAVE UDON AND... UDON AND...

H—

H-HELP ME!

A D-DEVIL SNATCHED MY DAUGHTER!

MY LITTLE GIRL, IT—

WHAT HAP-PENED?

I'M A PUBLIC SAFETY DEVIL HUNTER, SIR.

IT TOOK HER INTO THE WOODS!!

CURRY UDON'S UP!

IT'S DENJI!

WHAT'S YOUR NAME?

OH... THAT'S ME.

HUH?! UH, BUT I'M HAVING UDON TOO.

OKAY, DENJI...

I DON'T WANT MY NOODLES TO GET SOGGY. YOU GO KILL THE DEVIL BY YOURSELF.

REALLY?

PLEASE REMAIN INSIDE THE BUILDING FOR YOUR SAFETY.

AN EXPERIENCED DEVIL HUNTER IS ON THE JOB, SIR. HE'LL SAVE YOUR DAUGHTER.

WH... WHAT'S THAT MEAN...?

ONLY ANSWER WITH "YES" OR "WOOF."

DID YOU FORGET? YOU'RE MY PET.

I DON'T NEED A DOG WHO SAYS "NO."

...OUR USELESS DOGS GET EUTHANIZED.

I HEARD FROM AN ACQUAINTANCE IN THE CRIME SCENE DIVISION THAT...

YES'M.

WHAT'S YOUR ANSWER?

COME ON! THE UDON'LL GET SOGGY. OFF YOU GO!

I THOUGHT SHE WAS NICE.

I EVEN LIKED HER A LITTLE.

TREATIN' ME LIKE A DAMN DOG...!

I CAN'T BELIEVE SHE WAS THAT SCARY!

Woof!

I JUST REMEMBERED POCHITA'S *DEAD*...

BLAAAH...

HA HA!

AH HA HA HA!

AH.

OH, PLEASE! LET THIS DEVIL GO!

WAIT, WHAT?

WHEN HE WAS HITTING ME IN THE PARKING LOT TODAY...

...THIS NICE DEVIL SAVED ME!

MY DADDY... WHEN HE HAS A BAD DAY, HE *BEATS* ME.

SO, PLEASE! DON'T KILL HIM...

OUR USELESS DOGS GET EUTHANIZED.

I WAS BUDDIES WITH A DEVIL TOO. I KNOW...

...THERE ARE GOOD DEVILS.

HUH?

HEY... WANNA RUN AWAY TOGETHER? THE THREE OF US...?

SO DO YOU WANNA RUN AWAY...?

BUT IF I LET THIS DEVIL GO, THEY'RE GONNA KILL ME.

topple

YOU OKAY?

SHE SMELLS GOOD...

UH-OH.

WHUMP

SORRY... I END UP CUTTING MY OWN BODY WITH THE CHAINSAWS TOO...

LOOKS LIKE I LOSE TOO MUCH BLOOD AND GET FAINT...

HOW DID YOUR BODY END UP LIKE THAT?

MY PET DEVIL BECAME MY HEART.

UNBE-LIEVABLE, RIGHT?

THAT POCHITA DIED FOR ME...

I DON'T WANNA BELIEVE IT EITHER.

HISTORICALLY SPEAKING, YOUR CONDITION HAS VERY FEW PRE-CEDENTS.

SO FEW IT HASN'T EVEN BEEN NAMED.

SO I CAN TELL.

I HAVE AN ESPECIALLY GOOD NOSE.

I BELIEVE YOU.

YOUR BODY HAS *TWO* SCENTS. HUMAN *AND* DEVIL.

AND NOT IN THE POETIC SENSE...

YOUR BEST FRIEND IS STILL ALIVE INSIDE YOU.

OKAY...

WOW...

THAT'S A HUGE RELIEF!

I'LL EAT THAT UDON ...

I CA—

I CAN'T.

CAN YOU FEED YOUR-SELF?

YOU LOOK UNSTEADY.

gurgle

MAKIMA.

WHAT'S YOUR NAME...?

HEY, UH!

WHAT TYPE OF GUY DO YOU LIKE?

W...

MISS MAKIMA ---

HMMM....

WHAT TYPE OF GUY DO YOU LIKE?

SOMEONE LIKE THIS BOY NAMED DENJI.

ME TOO... I LIKE YOU TOO, MISS MAKIMA...

DENJI! OVER HERE!

ONCE YOU'RE CHANGED, I'LL INTRODUCE YOU TO ONE OF YOUR COLLEAGUES.

YES ?!

DENJI.

WE TYPICALLY WORK IN UNIFORM. PUT THIS ON.

FOR TODAY, TAG ALONG WITH HIM.

HE'S THREE YEARS YOUR SENIOR HERE.

THIS IS *AKI HAYA-KAWA.*

OF COURSE NOT.

I'M NOT WORKING WITH YOU, MISS MAKIMA?

Nooo! Miss Maki-maaa!!

YOU AND MISS MAKIMA ARE IN COMPLETELY DIFFERENT LEAGUES.

WE'RE GOING ON PATROL.

IF YOU PERFORM WELL, WE'LL BE ABLE TO WORK TOGETHER.

SO KEEP YOUR CHIN UP, OKAY?

IF YOU SHOW UP TOMORROW, I'LL GIVE YOU ANOTHER THRASHING.

YOU SHOULD QUIT.

MAYBE MY KINDNESS ISN'T GETTING THROUGH TO YOU...

WHAT'S YOUR PROBLEM...?

THE ONLY ONES STILL ALIVE ARE THOSE WHO HAVE STRONG CONVICTION.

AMONG MY PEERS, THE ONES WHO BECAME DEVIL HUNTERS JUST FOR THE MONEY GOT KILLED BY DEVILS. ALL OF THEM.

THE PEOPLE WHO GO INTO THIS JOB FOR SHALLOW REASONS END UP *DEAD*, KID.

DING DIIING.

THEN I WAS RIGHT TO BEAT YOU UP.

LEMME GUESS. YOU BECAME A DEVIL HUNTER CUZ YOU'VE GOT YOUR EYE ON MAKIMA?

...YOU GOT SCARED OF A DEVIL AND RAN AWAY.

I'LL DO YOU A FAVOR AND TELL MAKIMA...

YOU SURE ARE A NICE GUY...

WHAK WHAK WHAK WHAK

ONLY! I! AIM FOR! THE CROTCH! GUYS! WHEN I! FIGHT!

WHAK WHAK WHAK WHAK

huff huff

WHEW!

AND A HOT DOG TOO....

TODAY, I ATE UDON FOR THE *FIRST* TIME...

MY LIFE ISN'T MINE ALONE.

ACTUALLY, I TAKE THAT BACK.

GFF!

DO
NG

BO
W

YOU JUST WANT HER FOR YOURSELF!!

HUH?! WHAT GIVES?!

...HAS NO PLACE LIKING MAKIMA!

A THUG LIKE YOU...

THUD

YOU... SERIOUSLY...

...ONLY AIM FOR...

...THE BALLS...

CRAP.

A **TESTICLE DEVIL** ATTACKED HIS BALLS.

THAT'S A LIE... HE MADE THAT UP...

CAN YOU GET ALONG?

SO WHAT DO YOU THINK?

HMMM.

THIS GUY IS SCUM...

NOT A CHANCE.

I'M GLAD YOU GUYS ARE HITTING IT OFF.

THIS THUG?! REALLY?!

Squad?

BUT WE ALREADY HAVE SO MANY TROUBLE-MAKERS AS IT IS!

IF WE ADD ANY MORE WEIRDOS...

I'M PUTTING DENJI IN YOUR SQUAD, HAYAKAWA.

THAT I'D TRY OPERATING IT WITH A UNIQUE EXPERIMENTAL SETUP.

I TOLD YOU WHEN WE CREATED YOUR SQUAD, DIDN'T I?

JUST WHO IS THIS GUY?

DENJI HERE IS HUMAN, BUT HE CAN TURN INTO A DEVIL.

ARE YOU SERIOUS?

I'VE ONLY HEARD FLIMSY RUMORS ABOUT CASES LIKE THAT...

HOW DO YOU LIKE THAT?! BADASS, RIGHT?!

SO IT'S BEEN DECIDED THAT WE'LL TREAT HIM AS A SPECIAL CASE.

DENJI IS SPECIAL.

IF DENJI EVER QUITS OR DISOBEYS ORDERS...

...HE'LL BE PUT DOWN AS A DEVIL.

IT MEANS WE'LL BE WORKING TOGETHER UNTIL DEATH DO US PART.

WAIT... WHAT'S THAT MEAN?

FYI, THEY TOLD ME I CAN KILL YOU IF YOU RUN AWAY.

TURNS OUT YOU'RE GONNA LIVE WITH ME SO WE CAN KEEP AN EYE ON YOU.

IS MAKIMA A BAD PERSON?

HEY...

THEN IS SHE A GOOD PERSON?

IF YOU'RE A DEVIL, JUST BE GRATEFUL WE'RE LETTING YOU LIVE.

WE'RE DEVIL HUNTERS, REMEMBER?

IF YOU THINK SO, THEN GIVE UP ON HER.

OF COURSE SHE'S A GOOD PERSON...

I OWE HER MY LIFE...

Chain
saw
man

Chapter 4: Power

AND THE ULTIMATE BREAD IS READY!

STRAWBERRY JAM, PLUM JAM, MARMALADE AAAND...

...BUTTER AND HONEYYY AND... SHAKE SOME CINNAMON ON THERE TOO.

Mm!

PAID DAYS OFF, HUH-HUMM HUH-HUMM-HUM HUH-HUMM HUH-HUMM HUM!

UNION JOB, HUMM HUH-HUMM HUH HUH HUH HUH-HUMM!

You're taking too long in the bath!

Don't sleep on the toilet!

WE'VE GOT A *FIEND* INSIDE AN EAST NERIMA RESIDENCE.

CIVILIAN EVACUATION AND LOCKDOWN OF THE SCENE IS COMPLETE AT THIS TIME.

THE FIEND TARGET IS HOLED UP IN A ROOM ON THE SECOND FLOOR.

WE'LL LET YOU DEVIL HUNTERS HANDLE THE REST.

MR. HAYAKAWA, IS THAT A NEWBIE WITH YOU?

WHAT? DIDN'T YOU LEARN ANYTHING IN SCHOOL?

NOPE, DIDN'T GO TO SCHOOL.

HEY, WHAT'S A FIEND?

9ch

ak

THEN AREN'T I ONE?

OH REALLY? UH...

OHH.

A DEVIL THAT'S TAKEN OVER A PERSON'S CORPSE...

THAT'S A FIEND.

NO.

THEIR HEADS HAVE DISTINCT SHAPES.

WH

AM

WELL, YOU'LL UNDERSTAND WHEN YOU SEE ONE.

TURN INTO A DEVIL. SHOW ME YOUR POWER.

I'LL DECIDE WHETHER YOU'RE USE-FUL OR NOT.

YOU KILL THIS ONE.

FIENDS HAVE THE DEVIL'S PERSON-ALITY.

LISTEN UP. DON'T YOU FORGET THIS.

FIENDS ARE BONA FIDE DEVILS TOO.

A DEVIL HUNTER SHOULDN'T BE SYMPATHIZING WITH DEVILS.

BANG

MY ENTIRE FAMILY WAS KILLED BY A DEVIL RIGHT BEFORE MY EYES.

THE COPS DOWN THERE? I'VE GONE DRINKING WITH THEM BEFORE.

THEY'RE RISKING THEIR LIVES TO DO THEIR JOBS, TO PROTECT THEIR WIVES AND KIDS.

EVERYONE IS SERIOUS ABOUT THIS BUT YOU.

WHAT DO YOU WANT? TO BE FRIENDS WITH THEM?

I WANT TO KILL DEVILS IN WAYS THAT CAUSE THEM TO SUFFER AS MUCH AS POSSIBLE.

CUZ I DON'T HAVE ANY FRIENDS...

IF THERE ARE DEVILS I COULD BE FRIENDS WITH, THEN YEAH, I DO.

I'LL REMEMBER THOSE WORDS...

SLAM

BLAAAH... HE SURE HAS A SHORT TEMPER...

THE TRUTH IS, I JUST DIDN'T WANNA GET BLOOD ON THESE DIRTY MAGAZINES...

CUZ WITH THE CHAINSAWS, BLOOD ENDS UP SPRAYING ALL OVER.

I DID YOU A FAVOR KILLING YOU QUICK, SO I'M TAKING THESE!

ALL Right! Sexiness confirmed!

flip

SHOW ME YOUR DREAMS.

I'M SERIOUS ABOUT THIS TOO, POCHITA.

I'M LIVING A DREAM LIFE, JUST LIKE IN OUR CONTRACT, AREN'T I?

HE'S STILL CHASING HIS.

IT'S JUST THAT I'VE ALREADY CROSSED THE FINISH LINE TO MY DREAM.

WITH A PRETTY GIRL CLOSE BY...

I GET TO BATHE EVERY DAY.

AND EAT GOOD FOOD.

FOR THE GUYS BELOW, IT'S PROTECTING THEIR FAMILIES.

I BET HIS ULTIMATE GOAL IS A REVENGE THING.

I HAVE A FULL LIFE NOW... BUT IT DOES KINDA FEEL LIKE SOMETHING'S MISSING.

WAS THERE SOMETHING ELSE? MY REAL, TRUE GOAL...?

DOES MAKIMA HAVE ONE TOO?

DOES MAKIMA ALSO...

I GAVE UP ON IT FOREVER AGO CUZ I THOUGHT IT WAS IMPOSSIBLE FOR ME...

BUT I HAVE A DECENT JOB NOW. COULDN'T I DO IT?

JUMPING STRAIGHT TO SLEEPING WITH A WOMAN WOULD BE TOUGH FOR ME...

BUT IF IT'S BOOBS ...

IF IT'S BOOBS, IF I'VE GOT A STRONG WILL AND INITIATIVE, COULDN'T I TOUCH THEM...?

SO THAT'S WHAT HE MEANT! I'VE FOUND IT, DUDE...

IT'S....!

MY GOAL!

WHAT I'M SERIOUS ABOUT!

EVERYONE IS SERIOUS ABOUT THIS BUT YOU.

A BUDDY ---?

I'M PAIRING YOU UP WITH A BUDDY STARTING TODAY.

MAKIMA SAID SHE LIKED ME... BUT...

...IF I ASK TO TOUCH HER CHEST, THERE'S A CHANCE SHE'LL HATE ME...

PERFECT TIMING— LOOKS LIKE YOUR BUDDY'S HERE.

IN PUBLIC SAFETY, FOR SMALL-SCALE MISSIONS, PATROLLING AND SO ON, WE ACT IN PAIRS FOR SAFETY'S SAKE.

BE CARE-FUL...

SHE'S A FIEND.

C
h
a
i
n
s
a
w

m
a
n

Chapter 5:
A Way to Touch Some Boobs

BUT POWER HAS HIGH MENTAL FACULTIES, SO I PUT HER IN HAYAKAWA'S SQUAD.

FIENDS ARE TARGETS FOR EXTERMIN-ATION, SAME AS DEVILS.

HER HORNS WILL ATTRACT ATTENTION, SO ONLY PATROL PLACES WITH LITTLE TRAFFIC.

We're with Public Safety Devil Exter-mination Special Division 4, SIRRRS.

IF YOU RUN INTO ANY CIVILIAN DEVIL HUNTERS, OR GET QUESTIONED BY THE POLICE...

THERE aren't any Devils at all!

WAIT, WHAT?!

THEN HOW ARE WE GOING TO DELIVER RESULTS?!

THE NOBODY DEVILS ALL FLEE FROM MY SCENT, I'M SURE!

BEFORE I BECAME A FIEND, I WAS A GREATLY FEARED DEVIL!

LIKELY BECAUSE OF *ME*!

IF YOU HAVE ANY QUESTIONS, ASK HAYAKAWA.

HE'S THE ONE WHO PAIRED YOU TWO UP.

HE TEAMED ME UP WITH POWER TO KEEP ME FROM SHOWING WHAT I GOT.

HE'S TRYING TO FORCE ME OUT!

THAT JERK... HE SET ME UP, DIDN'T HE?!

I SMELL BLOOD!!

HEY! WHOA, WHOA, WHOA! WHERE DO YOU THINK YOU'RE GOING?!

FIGHT TIME! FIGHT TIME! BATTLE TIME!

SHE'S FAST!

Exci–?!

POWER, SINCE YOU WERE THE *BLOOD DEVIL* BEFORE YOU BECAME A FIEND, BATTLING USING BLOOD IS YOUR SPECIALTY...

...BUT YOU'RE SO EXCITABLE... MAYBE YOU WEREN'T CUT OUT TO BE A DEVIL HUNTER?

HUH ?!

THIS GUY SAID TO KILL IT, HE DID!

THISH–

HUH...?!

I-I CAN!

CAN YOU BE QUIET?

GOOD GIRL, POWER.

I WANT TO SEE BIG THINGS FROM YOU TWO.

HONESTLY, I DON'T REALLY CARE WHICH OF YOU WAS AT FAULT.

I'LL SH—! SH-SHOW YOU!

DO YOU THINK YOU CAN SHOW ME THAT?

MAYBE THIS ISN'T THE TIME TO BE THINKING ABOUT TOUCHING BOOBS.

MEOOOW!

STILL, I CAN'T WORK WITH SOME LIAR CHICK...

GETTING TO HAVE SOFT DRINKS IS, LIKE, A DREAM COME TRUE TO ME.

BUT IF WE KEEP SCREWING UP, IT'LL BE WAY WORSE THAN NOT GETTING TO HAVE SOFT DRINKS ANYMORE!

FOR A CAT? THAT'S STUPID!

I'D DO ANYTHING TO TOUCH SOME BOOBS THOUGH.

I DOUBT YOU'D UNDERSTAND SUCH SENTIMENT FOR THE LIKES OF A CAT.

IF I COULD JUST GET MEOWY BACK FROM THAT DEVIL, I'D DO ANYTHING— EVEN ALLY WITH A HUMAN!

...IF YOU GOT MEOWY BACK FROM THAT DEVIL FOR ME?

WHAT IF I SAID I'D LET YOU TOUCH MY CHEST...

HMM ---

OH, BUT IF IT WAS A *DOG*, I MIGHT GET IT...

SURE ENOUGH, I CAN'T COMPREHEND HUMANS.

HOW DARE...

...THEY KIDNAP A POOR CAT!!

OHH?!

THAT DAMN DEVIL!

OHH?

C h a i n

s a w

m a n

YOU CAN'T EVEN GO OUT ON YOUR OWN?

NOPE. I WAS SO BORED BEING IN HERE ALL THE TIME.

BE BACK BY FIVE O'CLOCK!

YOUR DAY-LEAVE REQUEST FOR THE FIEND POWER IS APPROVED.

Chapter 6: Service

THE PROBLEM IS THAT ONLY *YOU* CAN FIGHT IT.

THEN IT WOULD BE CHECK-MATE!

IF IT SEES *ME*, IT'LL USE MEOWY AS A SHIELD.

I KNOW WHERE TO FIND THE DEVIL WHO TOOK MEOWY!

CUZ HE'S ALIVE INSIDE ME, RIGHT IN HERE!

I CAN'T EVER PET HIM AGAIN, BUT IT'S OKAY.

HUMANS ARE SO FOOLISH!

I HAD A PET TOO. THIS DEVIL NAMED POCHITA.

THAT MEANS POCHITA DIED, DOES IT NOT?

THE DEAD HAVE NO LIFE!

"THEY'RE IN MY HEART" OR WHATEVER— THAT'S PATHETIC CONSOLATION!

SAY WHAT?

Chapter 6: Service

YEAH, YEAH... YOU'RE SO RIGHT.

THERE'S NOOO WAY I CAN BE FRIENDS WITH THIS CHICK.

THE SOVIET WAR HAWKS ARE GETTING LOUDER OVER THE AMERICAN MATTER.

WE'RE ALSO HEARING RUMORS THAT THEY'RE USING DEVILS FOR MILITARY PURPOSES.

MAKIMA... ARE THE DOGS IN THE SQUAD WE GAVE YOU COMING ALONG...?

WE CAN ONLY PRAY THAT THE DEVILS REMAIN JAPAN'S ONLY ENEMIES.

I HAVE ONE DOG THAT'S PROMIS-ING...

...AND ONE THAT'S INTER-ESTING.

ta

P

A PUPPY I RECENTLY TOOK IN.

INTER-ESTING ...?

BE SURE NOT TO GET ATTACHED.

YOUR JOB IS TO TRAIN DOGS AND USE THEM.

SL AM

ALL DEVILS ARE BORN WITH A NAME.

WHY DO YOU HAVE SUCH HIGH HOPES FOR HIM?

DENJI IS DISGUSTING. THERE'S NOTHING INTERESTING ABOUT HIM.

THE MORE THAT NAME IS FEARED, THE MORE POWERFUL THE DEVIL ITSELF.

BUT WHAT IF THERE WAS A *CAR DEVIL?* THAT CONJURES UP THE MENTAL IMAGE OF GETTING RUN OVER AND DYING, SO THAT MIGHT BE STRONG.

COFFEE HAS NO SCARY MENTAL IMAGE WHATSOEVER. IF THERE WAS A *COFFEE DEVIL,* IT WOULD PROBABLY BE WEAK.

DENJI CAN TURN INTO THE *CHAINSAW DEVIL.*

I REALLY DO THINK THAT'S INTERESTING.

IT'S INTERESTING AND NOTHING MORE. HE'S USELESS.

HE ISN'T FIT FOR PUBLIC SAFETY.

BUT HIM, HE SAID ALL HE WANTS IS TO LIVE THE EASY LIFE.

ONLY PEOPLE WITH GOALS OR CONVICTION SERVE IN PUBLIC SAFETY.

NOT TO MENTION HE THINKS YOU CAN BECOME *FRIENDS* WITH DEVILS.

HE'S STILL A BRAT.

JUST SOME BRAT.

HUMAN JESTS ARE SO UNAMUS-ING!

HUH?

YEAH? WHAT IS IT?

STORY?

OHH? WAS THAT MY STORY?

ISN'T IT GONNA USE YOUR CAT AS A HOSTAGE IF YOU SHOW UP?

YOU CAN'T COME THIS CLOSE WITH ME, RIGHT?

HE'S A FOOL, BUT HE HAD GOOD INTUITION...

UGH!

UHN...

SL AM

I HAD TO WAIT THAT LONG TILL I COULD FINALLY GET OUTSIDE TOO!

DON'T COMPLAIN!

YOU MADE ME WAIT FOR QUITE SOME TIME, BLOOD DEVIL...

I THOUGHT YOU'D RUN AWAY...

GAH!

THIS INFERNAL WOUND FORCED ME TO HIDE MY GRAND SELF!

LOOK AT MY ARM, HUMAN! YOU DAMN HUMANS DID THIS TO ME!

LIKE I CARE, IDIOT!

...SO I'LL HEAL IT WITH HUMAN BLOOD!

HUMANS CARVED THIS WOUND UPON ME...

MY MEAL BARKS!

BAT DEVIL !!

I BROUGHT YOU A HUMAN AS PROMISED!

NOW GIVE MEOWY BACK!

AH, YES... WAS THAT THE DEAL?

HRRM ?

gulp

YOU SAID
YOU CAN'T
PET POCHITA
ANYMORE...

THERE WAS THIS ONE TIME POCHITA WENT MISSING.

BUT WHEN I GOT HOME, POCHITA WAS THERE WAITING FOR ME, CRYING.

I THOUGHT HE'D BEEN EATEN BY A DEVIL...

I LOOKED ALL OVER TOWN AND STILL COULDN'T FIND 'IM.

POCHITA WASN'T THERE WHEN I WOKE UP.

I REMEMBER BEING SO RELIEVED THAT WE FELL ASLEEP TOGETHER RIGHT ON THE SPOT.

...HOW DID SHE FEEL WHEN SHE WENT TO SLEEP AT NIGHT?

AFTER MEOWY GOT TAKEN BY A DEVIL...

TO BE CONTINUED...

Chain
saw

man

YOU'RE READING THE WRONG WAY!

Chainsaw Man reads from right to left, starting in the upper-right corner. Japanese is read from right to left, meaning that action, sound effects and word-balloon order are completely reversed from English order.